Original title:
Poems from the Pulpwood

Copyright © 2025 Creative Arts Management OÜ
All rights reserved.

Author: Samuel Kensington
ISBN HARDBACK: 978-1-80567-291-3
ISBN PAPERBACK: 978-1-80567-590-7

Kinship with the Canopy

In the trees, a family grows,
Squirrels throw acorns, who knows?
A raccoon in a tux spins around,
Under twinkling leaves, laughter's found.

Frogs in bowties croak a tune,
While owls silently swoon at the moon.
Branches wiggle like dancers in glee,
Root yourself here; you'll see what I see.

Nature's Narrative in Grain

Woodpeckers drum a zany beat,
Each thunk on the trunk, a rhythmic treat.
Ants in line, a marching brigade,
They laugh as they go, their plans never fade.

A beaver's a builder, a branching old chap,
Constructing a dam with a splash and a flap.
Beneath the bark, tales twist and twirl,
In nature's wild dance, watch the shavings unfurl.

Songs from the Spruce

On spruce branches, laughter soars,
With giggling birds that play games galore.
A deer prances by, dressed in style,
With a grin like a star, it stops for a while.

The wind sings secrets through needle-thin leaves,
Tickling the pinecones, where laughter weaves.
A rabbit hops by, wearing spectacles too,
In this woodland concert, it's all about you.

The Echo of Elms

In the elms, whispers travel far,
Echoes of giggles from the squirrels' bazaar.
A raccoon's prank shakes the trunk just right,
While shadows clap hands in the soft twilight.

A blue jay sings jokes that never tire,
As the sun dips low, they dance by the fire.
Each rustle and chuckle in the cool evening air,
Brings joy to the trees, a whimsical affair.

The Lure of the Leaf

A leaf once told me a joke,
It fell with laughter, a prank so broke.
It danced on air, a whimsical flight,
Chasing the wind, oh what a sight!

The squirrels chuckled, tails in a fluff,
While birds chimed in, saying, "That's enough!"
But the leaf just giggled, swirled with glee,
In a world where comedy's free as can be.

Treetop Treasures

In the treetops, a pirate ship wails,
With acorn treasure and whimsical tales.
The branches sway in a jig and a stomp,
As chipmunks plot a plunderous romp.

With every gust, the laughter does soar,
As they search for bounty at nature's door.
A parrot squawks, "Yo ho, my friend!"
In this leafy realm, the fun never ends.

Atmospheric Canopies

Beneath the ceiling of leaves so green,
The skylight whispers where few have been.
The crickets serenade in a funny tune,
Under the watch of a piebald moon.

Dandelions giggle in a breezy dance,
While clouds overhead seem to glance askance.
With ups and downs, the weather plays tricks,
In this canopy realm, pure joy often flicks.

The Dance of the Driftwood

On the riverbank, driftwood holds court,
Telling tall tales of its water-bound sport.
Each piece a character, with stories to spin,
As otters chuckle, inviting you in.

The current twirls them, a rollicking play,
While frogs add vocals to the love of the day.
"Woot! Woot!" the driftwood cries with delight,
In a festival of fun under starry night.

Serene Saplings and Stories

In a forest so wide, with leaves that jest,
Little saplings giggle, they can't help but rest.
The squirrel tells tales with a flick of his tail,
While birds play charades, a comedic trail.

A tree once told me it yearns for a hat,
To keep off the rain and combat the chat.
With roots in mischief and branches in glee,
These saplings spin yarns, a sight to see!

Tapestry of Bark and Branch

In the tapestry woven of bark and of twist,
Branches conspire, they just can't resist.
A knotted old tree, with a wise, crackled grin,
Claims every lost acorn is where he's been.

The owls wear their glasses, all up in a fuss,
While rabbits play poker, oh what a plus!
They roll with the wind, in a dance quite absurd,
As nature's own jesters, they never felt heard.

The Song of the Sawdust

In the workshop, a melody's found in the grind,
The sawdust is singing, oh what a find!
With every sharp cut, it hums a new tune,
The hammers join in, a crafty cartoon.

Chairs chat with tables, in witty debate,
While benches play matchmaker, setting up fate.
The wood's filled with laughter, a joyous embrace,
As each bit of sawdust just dances in place.

Heartwood Dreams

In dreams of the heartwood where secrets lie deep,
The trees whisper jokes, they'll help you lose sleep.
With roots in the quirkiness, branches ask why,
While shadows break into laughter that flies.

Each ring tells a story, a punchline at best,
As barks boast of ages, in jest they invest.
The forest is vibrant, with humor abound,
In heartwood's embrace, pure joy can be found.

Harvesting Dreams from Trees

In the forest, dreams take flight,
With squirrels debating day and night.
Acorns drop like little clowns,
Sprouting giggles from the towns.

A beaver's got a plan, oh dear,
Building castles, hoarding cheer.
Trees stretch tall, they bend and sway,
Whispering jokes in their own way.

Mushrooms tango on the ground,
While crickets laugh with a joyful sound.
Nature's circus, a grand display,
Harvesting dreams as they play away.

Flights of Fancy among the Foliage

Butterflies wear capes of glitter,
While the ants laugh, calling them quitter.
They flutter past the snickering bees,
Who buzz in rhythm, dancing with ease.

A ladybug juggles seeds, can you see?
Singing loudly, a tune of glee.
Frogs play cards by the pond so green,
With jokes about a king and his queen.

High up in branches, owls have a ball,
Whispering secrets, never too small.
In the foliage, fun never ends,
As the trees share tales with all their friends.

The Chronicles of Cedar

Cedar stands like a gnome so wise,
Telling tales of the evening skies.
Its branches wave, a friendly grin,
As raccoons plot their next cheeky win.

Squirrels throw shade as they chatter near,
While foxes play poker, fueled by cheer.
Cedar's wisdom echoes the night,
With giggles that twinkle, a pure delight.

The moon joins in, a sparkling sage,
Dancing with shadows upon the stage.
Whiskers and whiskers, it's a laugh fest,
In Cedar's shade, every critter's a guest.

Woodland Whimsy

In the woodland, whimsy reigns supreme,
Where every tree has a silly dream.
Mice perform in a tiny band,
While rabbits juggle with a steady hand.

The breeze carries laughter, soft and sweet,
As turtles kick back, taking a seat.
Fungi play hopscotch, mushrooms in line,
Racing the wind—oh, isn't it fine?

Giggling grubs slide down the bark,
Performing stunts from morning till dark.
In a world that's bursting with fun,
Woodland whimsy has just begun!

Shadows of Sturdy Giants

In the woods where shadows play,
Roots stretch like a giant's stay.
With hats of moss and shoes of mud,
They're the tallest friends who never bud.

They whisper jokes with every breeze,
Tickling branches, teasing leaves.
Telling tales of squirrels bold,
And of acorns that refuse to be sold.

Where Ferns Dance with Dreams

Ferns in a line, they shimmy and sway,
Ballet in green under skies of gray.
With tiny feet that skip and leap,
They dream of lands where giggles creep.

In this waltz, they twirl and spin,
With secret laughs buried within.
Each frond a song, each leaf a cheer,
Echoing laughter that only they hear.

The Language of Leaves

Leaves chatter in colors so bright,
Clapping hands in the soft daylight.
They gossip of ants and their clumsy race,
Telling tales with a flick and a trace.

When autumn comes, they make a scene,
Throwing shades of orange, red, and green.
Underfoot, they rustle a tune,
Singing loudly, "Goodbye, carefree June!"

Secrets Beneath the Bark

Beneath the bark where whispers creep,
A party of critters has gathered to peep.
With secrets stacked in each knotted groove,
They swap funny stories that make them move.

The beetles chuckle and crickets sing,
While mushrooms plot a mischievous thing.
In their cozy nook, laughter takes root,
It's a woodsy delight that's positively cute!

Reflections in the Riven Wood

In the woods where shadows dance,
A squirrel does a silly prance.
He trades his acorns for some cheese,
And giggles with the buzzing bees.

The trees are tall, their branches sway,
As critters gather, come what may.
A raccoon dons a funny hat,
While pondering where the snacks are at.

A wise old owl falls from his perch,
Declaring it's time for a lurch.
The forest floor, a stage for glee,
As laughter echoes, wild and free.

So when you stroll through leafy lanes,
Remember all the capers and gains.
For in this riven wood we find,
The joy that tickles every mind.

Chronicle of the Carver's Hand

A carver sat with knife in hand,
Crafting figures, oh so grand.
He whittled down a ducky grin,
Then lost his thumb while diving in.

His tools are spread like smelly cheese,
With shavings scattered in the breeze.
Each wobbly sheep he sends to fame,
As kids all giggle at his game.

A lumberjack gave him a cheer,
But slipped and fell, oh dear, oh dear!
The noise was loud, the laugh divine,
With every slip, the trees did pine.

The chronicles of wood and laughs,
Are filled with quirk and silly gaffs.
So when you see that carver there,
Join in the fun, show him you care.

Serenity in the Sylvan Silence

In the woods where whispers roam,
A frog decides he'll make a home.
He croaks a tune, it's quite a show,
While birds just shake their heads, you know.

A deer draped in a leafy crown,
Struts around, he wears a frown.
He stepped on gum, oh what a plight,
He hops away in sheer delight.

The squirrels hold a dance-off soon,
With acorn hats beneath the moon.
They spin and twirl, a merry band,
In a woodland workspace, oh so grand.

In the silence of the pines so tall,
Nature's giggles do enthrall.
For every treetop holds a jest,
In this serene and silly quest.

Tales from the Treehouse

Up in the branches high and wide,
A treehouse stands with glee and pride.
The kids all dream, they clap and shout,
For nonsense adventures, there's no doubt.

The raccoon plays the jester's role,
He spins a yarn, aims for the hole.
His tail is stuck, oh what a sight,
While laughter bubbles into the night.

The lemonade spills, a sticky stream,
As giggling friends hold tight to dreams.
They plot mischief under the stars,
Whispering tales of candy bars.

So climb the stairs to fun and play,
In the treehouse, where smiles stay.
For every tale is crafted fine,
With joy and laughter, so divine.

Rooted in Reverie

In a forest where squirrels smile,
Trees giggle, stacking leaves in a pile.
A raccoon juggling acorns with flair,
Leaves a forest deep in laughter and air.

Bees in bow ties humming their tune,
Chasing butterflies under the moon.
A woodpecker knocks on a joke-filled trunk,
While shadows of shrubs dance in a funk.

Mushrooms hold parties, a real funny scene,
Telling tales of the grass, quite keen.
In this wood where each whisper is bright,
Laughter echoes, a delightful sight.

So come, dear friend, join this cheer,
In roots of rev'y where giggles appear.
With every rustle and silly old pun,
Nature's jesters just want some fun.

Verses Entwined in Vines

Grapes are gossiping high in the leaves,
Climbing each other like old, funny thieves.
A chubby caterpillar laughs at its role,
As it wiggles along like a mischievous soul.

Lemons break dance in the summer sun,
While strawberries joke, saying, "This is fun!"
Vines twist and tangle in a silly embrace,
It's a vegetable fest at a fruity race.

The tomatoes are wearing their finest attire,
Celebrating life in the breeze, oh so dire.
A pumpkin jokes it's just been carved out,
Leaving us chuckling without any doubt.

So tiptoe through gardens where laughter is found,
In a place where the vines spin tales all around.
With each twist and turn, let mirth intertwine,
In this garden of giggles, imbibed with wine.

The Twisting Tales of Timber

In a deep, dark forest where branches bend,
The trees tell tales that never seem to end.
A cedar cracked jokes with a pine on the side,
While willows weaved whispers, their laughter wide.

Each twig is a storyteller, each leaf, a giggle,
In this woodland of humor, they wiggle and wiggle.
An old oak stands tall with a grin on its bark,
Sharing puns that ignite a joyful spark.

Squirrels hold court, passing acorns like gold,
"Who stole my last nut?" the stories unfold.
A fox in a hat sprinkles tales with delight,
Turning shadows to laughter, stretching out the night.

So listen closely beneath the leafy dome,
In the heart of the forest, humor calls it home.
With a chuckle and cheer from timber and tree,
You'll find the most spirited company.

Messages on the Maple

On a maple's branches, messages ride,
With leaves swapping secrets, side by side.
"Love is like syrup, sweet to the core!"
The laughter of autumn, who could ask for more?

A squirrel sent texts via acorn and bark,
Flirting with birds who just loved to embark.
"Meet me at sunset, let's swing from the dome,
With whispers of sweet dreams, we'll make it our home!"

Frogs croak in rhythm, a quirky old tune,
Jumping to laughter beneath the full moon.
"Life's like a maple, let your happiness flow,
With each leaf that falls, there's more room to grow."

So gather your friends, let the giggles begin,
Under the canopy where the silly wins.
In messages whispered on branches above,
Nature's a jokester, spreading the love.

Odes to the Old Growth

In the forest, trees stand tall,
Waving branches, having a ball.
Squirrels dance and make a fuss,
Chasing shadows, just because.

Mossy beards on limbs so grand,
Whisper secrets, hand in hand.
Old logs giggle, roots entwined,
Nature's jesters, fun defined.

Acorns drop, a playful fall,
Nutty caps that softly call.
Echoes of laughter in the air,
Woodland antics everywhere.

Trees share jokes, in rings they age,
Life's a show, and they're the stage.
Old growth grinning, leaf to leaf,
In the forest, joy's belief.

Through the Bedroom of Breezes

The wind whispers, soft and light,
Swaying curtains, a playful sight.
Breezes giggle, tickle the hair,
Ruffling sheets with a carefree flair.

Pillow fights with puffs of air,
Cushions bouncing everywhere.
Sunshine peeks through fluttering drapes,
Dancing shadows, funny shapes.

A squirrel sneaks in, quite the tease,
Skimming past with utmost ease.
Chasing dreams while breezes play,
In this room, joy finds a way.

Each gust brings a funny tale,
Of nature's antics, without fail.
In this space of laugh and cheer,
The bedroom of breezes, hold it dear.

An Arborist's Alchemy

With saw in hand and a grin so wide,
An arborist takes nature's ride.
Casting spells with every cut,
Turning stumps into laughter's rut.

Branches sway like floppy hats,
In his workshop, no room for spats.
Wood shavings dance, like tiny sprites,
Creating magic on those heights.

Logs transformed into silly sights,
Funky benches, quirky heights.
A treehouse that spins with delight,
Bringing joy both day and night.

The spells of trees, he knows them well,
With every chop, a story to tell.
In his realm of green and craft,
Laughter flows, a hearty laugh!

Trunk of Thought

In the heart of woods, thoughts take root,
The trunk of life, where dreams shoot.
Branches of ideas, spreading wide,
In the forest where jests reside.

Knots of wisdom, twisted tales,
Bark-covered laughter never fails.
Each ring a jest, a time well spent,
Life's a pun, and trees present.

Hollow logs echo with joyous glee,
Songs of the forest, wild and free.
The trunk stands steady, wise and bright,
Cracking jokes under the moonlight.

So lean in close, listen and hear,
Nature's laughter will bring you cheer.
In the woods where thoughts intertwine,
The trunk of humor, forever divine.

Harmony in the Hush of Woods

In dappled light where squirrels dance,
The trees debate, oh what a glance!
A crow caws loud, a twig does snap,
And laughter echoes, nature's clap.

Beneath the boughs, a rabbit sneezes,
While deer play tag on gentle breezes.
A chipmunk tells a joke so grand,
Yet no one hears, it's perfectly planned.

The owls hoot like they're in a band,
With nighttime beats that are quite unplanned.
They strut about, in shadows deep,
A woodland party — who needs sleep?

So here we sit, in leafy glades,
With silly thoughts and no charades.
The forest hums, a joyful tune,
In harmony — we all commune.

Juxtaposition of Juicy Sap

The maple tree wears a syrupy crown,
While the oak just laughs in its sturdy gown.
A squirrel's snack is nature's gift,
While bees buzz by, their wings adrift.

The sap drips down in sticky streams,
As pine trees plot their fragrant dreams.
A woodpecker taps, in rhythmic flair,
While branches sway, up in the air.

Laughter rises with the morning dew,
With nature's quirks, so fresh and new.
A chipmunk steals the scene with flair,
It twirls and dips without a care.

In this odd pairing, we find delight,
With every twist, a silly sight.
Each tree, each critter, plays a part,
In nature's orchestra, a merry heart.

Crafting with Nature's Heart

I found a twig, a sharp-witted spear,
And thought, why not, let's have some cheer!
With leaves and stones, a masterpiece,
A crown of flowers for my caprice.

A pinecone whisper, a secret sound,
As nature's treasures dance around.
I gather acorns, a quirky haul,
To decorate my woodland hall.

With mud for paste, and grass for glue,
I build a throne, as kings would do.
But when I sit, it starts to split,
Nature's giggle, I must admit.

So here I laugh, my project spun,
Crafting memories, silly fun.
For in the woods where wild things play,
Each quirky aspect brightens the day.

The Last Leaf Falls

A leaf once proud, now takes a dive,
It pirouettes, as if alive.
With a twist and turn, it hits the ground,
The forest giggles with the sound.

The branches wave, oh, what a scene!
"Come join the dance!" they laugh and preen.
As sunbeams tickle, the shadows play,
While breezes join the grand ballet.

Each flutter down is a comic skit,
As the last leaf falls, it gives a fit.
Then rolls away, a tumbleweed,
In autumn's grasp, a funny bead.

So let us muse, as seasons change,
With each new leaf, life's sweet exchange.
For laughter echoes in every fall,
Nature's whimsical, joyful call.

Timeless Whispers of the Timber

In the forest, trees play tricks,
With acorns dropped like little bricks.
Squirrels giggle, dodging flies,
As woodpeckers drum their alibis.

Branches sway with tales to tell,
Of secret parties in the dell.
Each leaf dances, joining cheer,
While the moss lounges without a fear.

Rabbits ponder their next stunt,
As the logs voice their playful grunt.
Nature's laughter bubbles bright,
In every bark, a hidden bite.

So, gather 'round the timber's cheer,
Where woodland whimsy grins sincere.
The whispers of the wood abound,
With humor in each sprightly sound.

The Call of the Cedar

Cedar calls, with a gentle sway,
Inviting critters to join the play.
A chipmunk hops, all dressed in stripes,
While the squirrels crack some nutty gripes.

Bark is thick but full of jokes,
As owls share wisdom with the folks.
A squirrel argues with the breeze,
Debating who is smarter—trees or bees?

With a wink, the branches nod,
Sharing giggles beneath the odd.
Nature's antics never fade,
Under this leafy masquerade.

In whispering winds around us flow,
The cedar's tales, they overflow.
Life's natural humor, never shy,
Is written in the clear blue sky.

Nature's Archive of Aromatic Air

In the air, aromas swirl,
From fragrant blooms, a dance unfurl.
Bees complain about their weight,
While daisies laugh, their gossip great.

Breezes carry scents of pine,
Mingling with mint, oh how divine!
Critters stop just to engage,
In this perfume, they find their stage.

Thyme and sage, they gossip loud,
Sprouting stories, feeling proud.
Nature's scents will leave a mark,
That tickle noses, spark a lark.

So take a whiff, your senses tease,
In fragrant fields, we find our ease.
Each whiff a tale, each scent a cheer,
In the archives of nature, joy is near.

The Artistry of the Aged Oak

The aged oak stands tall and wise,
With knots and bends like ancient ties.
It offers shade, a comfy seat,
For chipmunks who've just made their feat.

Boughs stretched wide, a canvas broad,
Painted leaves in their green facade.
Squirrels perform their acrobats,
Jumping high with little spats.

Roots and branches, a structure grand,
A playground for the frolic band.
A whispered joke, a playful jest,
The oak holds secrets, never guests.

So come and sit, enjoy the view,
With laughter echoing under blue.
In nature's art where joy's abound,
The aged oak, a throne profound.

Chants Among the Canopies

In the trees, the squirrels sing,
A melody of nuts and bling.
They chatter loud, they hoot and squeak,
In their world, it's quite the freak.

Birds shout tunes from high above,
While branches sway like they're in love.
The leaves dance to a haughty beat,
As critters join this wild retreat.

A raccoon plays a funky tune,
Underneath the glowing moon.
With acorns strewn as disco balls,
They boogie down within the sprawls.

Laughter echoes in the night,
As woodland critters take their flight.
In the canopy, the fun's not rare,
A circus up in leafy air.

Legends of the Leafy Realm

Once a tree grew very stout,
With rumors swirling all about.
It claimed a crown of leafy flair,
While neighboring trees grinned with despair.

The wise old owl chuckled low,
As squirrels gathered for the show.
'That tree thinks it's a big hotshot,
But it's just a lumbered knot!'

The raccoons dressed in finest wear,
Held a party with much flair.
In costumes made of bark and twine,
They toasted roots, 'Here's to the pine!'

Legends made with every jest,
In this realm, the trees invest.
With laughter shared from bough to bough,
There's more fun here than one could vow.

Dusk Chorus of the Deforest

When dusk falls, the croaks begin,
As frogs start their nightly din.
They croon in choruses galore,
While bats swoop down, seeking more.

Crickets chirp in fancy dress,
With tiny legs, they dance with zest.
The fireflies flash their neon light,
As shadows stir, preparing for flight.

The raccoons gather for the show,
To witness nature's evening glow.
They roll their eyes at the silly songs,
In their world, no one belongs.

A wise old tree snickers near,
As all the creatures find their cheer.
In dusk's embrace, let laughter flow,
For in the forest, joy will grow.

Revelations in Resin

In the forest's secret nook,
Trees hold stories in their book.
With sticky sap, they weave their tales,
Of woodland pals and windy gales.

A beaver grins with fervent glee,
For he's the king of timber spree.
He carves out stories, one by one,
In rings of resin, always fun.

The woodpecker's rhythmic knock
Announces gossip round the block.
Each tap reveals a juicy scoop,
As tousled critters form a group.

With resin pride, the trees confer,
In every drop, a giggle's stir.
Their laughter lingers in the breeze,
Crafting memories amongst the trees.

The Romance of Rains

Raindrops dance upon my head,
A tap-tap rhythm, joy instead.
My umbrella flies like a kite,
In this soggy, silly delight.

Puddles form like tiny pools,
With splashes, we embrace our fools.
Giggling kids in rubber boots,
As ducks parade in feathered suits.

The clouds above, a fluffy haze,
They grumble softly, growl, and praise.
With every drop, a joyous leap,
A love affair that's oh so deep.

In stormy weather, laughter reigns,
A quirky heart in playful chains.
So here's to rains, the love we find,
In every splash, a tale entwined.

Nature's Notebook

In the forest, whispers bloom,
Squirrels scribble in the gloom.
With tiny paws, they write their tales,
While dancing leaves catch breezy gales.

The frogs compose a croaky song,
In harmony, they all belong.
As bunnies pause to read their lines,
While porcupines sup on pines.

The sunshine spills on pages green,
Nature's verses, bright and keen.
With petals turned to magazines,
And tiny bugs in ragged jeans.

So take a peek at nature's lore,
With giggles sung, we can't ignore.
Each leaf a page, each breeze a quill,
In this wild world, we're laughing still.

Petals and Pulp Together

Petals soft like whispered wishes,
Joking with the puddle fishes.
In a paper mill, a floral ride,
Water and blooms, side by side.

The paper cranes want to soar,
But stumble on a flower's floor.
With every flap, they twist and turn,
In this floral dance, we learn.

Winds of chuckles pass the trees,
Where doodled dreams float like the bees.
Petals laugh, they pirouette,
In nature's paper ballet set.

Amidst the laughter and the paint,
A funny sight that won't grow faint.
Pulp and petals in a whirl,
Create a giggling, flowery swirl.

The Whisper of Wilderness

The trees confide in rustling tones,
With every breeze, a giggle moans.
The critters snicker, play their part,
In wild wilderness, we start.

The mountains chuckle, clouds in flight,
As shadows tease with playful fright.
A fox wearing spectacles and a crown,
Leads the parade through thickets brown.

Silly dances with deer and hare,
While mischievous raccoons declare,
That nature's law is laughter's thread,
In every nook where dreams are fed.

So roam the woods, full of cheer,
Where every whisper brings us near.
In wilderness, with joy we roam,
Finding funny tales we call home.

Echoing in the Grove

In the grove where the squirrels chatter,
Trees wear hats made of leaves that flatter.
The chipmunks dance in their tiny shoes,
While the owls chuckle at what they choose.

A raccoon tries his paw at a rhyme,
But all he finds is a can of thyme.
The singing frogs act like they're the band,
And the crickets clap with their tiny hands.

A parrot joins in, squawking away,
Forgetting the lyrics, he just wants to play.
His feathers bright, a carnival sight,
In this woodland show, everything's light.

The trees lean close, they're dying to hear,
The tales of a snail who dreams without fear.
With giggles and wiggles, they join the fun,
For in this grove, all animals run!

The Poetry of the Pine

Pines write verses that tickle the breeze,
Their needles whisper secrets with ease.
The pine cones fall, and it's quite a sight,
As they bounce around in a humorous flight.

A woodpecker taps, keeping perfect time,
While the sunbeams dance, creating a rhyme.
The wise old owl sits on a bough,
Laughing at all the antics, somehow.

The branches sway as they join the song,
Grumbling about how life can be long.
The forest is rich with laughter and cheer,
Especially when all of nature's near.

From the high to the low, the giggles we hear,
For the pines have secrets that make us all cheer.
In this realm of green, there's nothing quite fine,
As we celebrate the quirky poetry of pine.

Gargantuan Guardians of Green

Standing high, the giants all grin,
With faces carved by ages within.
Each tree a story, with bark that is wise,
Their laughter echoes under sunny skies.

The rabbits hop, full of mischief and glee,
With tales of adventure that you would agree.
A sloth in a hammock, just hanging around,
His jokes slow-dance with the leaves on the ground.

As seasons change, they wear new attire,
With colors so vivid, it never gets dire.
The acorns fall like confetti from above,
Celebrating the beauty, the laughter, the love.

With roots intertwined, they share their old tales,
Filling the forest with giggles like gales.
The guardians laugh with their hearts wide open,
In the land of the green, their joy is unbroken.

Seasons in the Silhouette

As autumn leaves twist in the air,
The trees tell stories without a care.
With winter's chill, they bundle tight,
Exchanging jokes in the pale moonlight.

Spring bursts forth with a crazy dance,
Where flowers giggle and bees prance.
Summer sun raises a fun debate,
About which fairy can carry the weight.

The moon takes bets on who will win,
As the crickets chirp with a sly little grin.
Seasons change, and the laughter flows,
In silhouettes where joy always grows.

Nature's rhythm, a hilarious beat,
With each twist and turn, a fun little treat.
In this land of colors, so vivid and bright,
The seasons perform in pure delight.

Starlight Through the Spruce

Midnight snickers, crickets laugh,
A squirrel's dance, a silly gaffe.
Frogs in tuxedos croaking bold,
Under starlight, stories told.

Mice with capes, they take a flight,
Swinging low from branches light.
A shadowed fox in fuzzy socks,
Chases fireflies, slips on rocks.

The owl hoots out a punchline sly,
While raccoons join, oh my, oh my!
With twinkling eyes, the fawns all prance,
Under the moon, they laugh and dance.

Through spruce and laughter, the night goes on,
Jokes in whispers till the dawn.
The forest giggles, wild and free,
In the starlit joy, we find glee.

Whispers of the Woodland

In the woodland where whispers play,
Trees gossip like friends at a cafe.
A woodpecker taps with a snarky tone,
While ants march by, each bearing a cone.

Bunny rabbits plot their next big feat,
A hopping contest, such a treat!
Amid the ferns, they giggle and cheer,
Planning for carrots with a pint of beer.

Squirrels on branches, so bold and spry,
Confessing secrets as leaves flutter by.
Chipmunks snicker, tails in the air,
About lost acorns and being a pair.

The forest hums with laughter galore,
Each creature's joke we can't ignore.
In whispers of joy, the world takes flight,
Of woodland wonders and pure delight.

Echoes of the Timber

In timbered halls where echoes play,
Trees tell tales, come what may.
A bear sings high, out of his range,
While rabbits giggle, it's quite the change.

Branches sway to a rhythm sweet,
As mockingbirds chirp with a witty beat.
A dance off starts, under moonlit beams,
The logs roll on, defying dreams.

Beneath the boughs, a kooky scene,
With badger jugglers, oh what a routine!
The shadows twirl in a merry jest,
As laughter echoes, this night's the best.

In timber's embrace, we laugh away,
Nature's humor, come what may.
With each echo, joy spreads wide,
In the mighty woods, laughter can't hide.

Beneath the Canopy's Embrace

Beneath the canopy, where shadows frolic,
The trees tell stories, some are symbolic.
A prancing deer in a tutu bright,
Dances through patches of dappled light.

The mushrooms giggle, in colors so bold,
Sharing secrets, some silly, some old.
Wise old owls with glasses perched right,
Crack jokes that make us laugh, what a sight!

With squirrel acrobats swinging high,
The woodland stage is the limit, oh my!
And in this charm, nature's own farce,
We gather by moonlight, the ultimate farce.

Under leaves, we find this joy,
Where whimsy reigns, every girl and boy.
In the embrace of green, forever we'll stay,
Laughter and mirth lead the way.

Shadows of the Felled Forest

In the wood where shadows creep,
Fallen trees lay fast asleep.
Squirrels plot with flying glee,
Using bark as a bouncy spree.

Branches joke with silly swings,
And the chirpy birdie sings.
Mice wear hats made of fine leaves,
While chipmunks play their silly thieves.

Roots that tangle, roots that trip,
Fumbles turn into a flip.
Laughter echoes through the air,
While trees chuckle without a care.

Nature's jesters, grand and bold,
Tales of laughter to be told.
In a world of green and wood,
The forest laughs, misunderstood.

The Dance of the Dappled Light

Sunbeams bounce on branches high,
Like little dancers in the sky.
Leaves join in with a twirl and twist,
In the forest, none can resist.

Mossy stones keep the beat,
While shadows shuffle on their feet.
Bees and butterflies do a jig,
As the sun performs a gig.

Every glimmer holds a flair,
Rustling leaves, no cares, no pair.
The dappled light begins to sway,
Nature's party, come what may.

When night falls, it's no dampener,
Moonlight joins, a smooth enhancer.
The dance of friends both day and night,
In the woods, all's pure delight.

Nostalgia of the Knotty Pine

Knotty pine with tales to tell,
Remembers when it knew so well.
Boys would climb and swing so free,
Hopeful hearts on branches, glee.

Sawdust dreams in summer's haze,
Resin scents from childhood days.
Now it wobbles, old and wise,
Wears a crown of bustling flies.

Echoed laughter in the breeze,
Ghosts of friends - oh, if you please!
Knotty pine with a cheeky grin,
Sipping sunshine, inviting in.

Every knot a memory stowed,
Wandering paths where laughter flowed.
In its shade, the worlds unite,
A haven filled with pure delight.

Threads of Twisted Roots

Twisted roots with wishes bound,
Tangles where the laughter's found.
They trip up gnomes and dance with elves,
Helping dreams to find themselves.

Worms giggle in their earthy lanes,
Tickling toes while dropping rains.
Frogs in hats add to the fun,
Belting croaks like they're the sun!

Each curve tells a tale unclear,
Of mischief done and brewed-up cheer.
Roots entwined like friendships grow,
In every twist, a grin will show.

Underneath, a party swells,
With teasing whispers, twisted spells.
Join the roots, clap feet to floor,
In nature's joy, we all explore!

Beneath Boughs and Blossoms

In the shade where squirrels play,
Beneath the leaves they twist and sway.
Chasing tails with silly cheer,
Laughs echo, spreading far and near.

Flowers giggle, petals bright,
Dancing with the ants in flight.
A rabbit hops, a clumsy feat,
Tripping over his own two feet.

The bees debate on who's the best,
While butterflies just take their rest.
The sun shines down with warming grin,
Nature's voice sings sweet within.

So if you wander beneath these trees,
Join the fun, feel the breeze.
For laughter blooms where life's a show,
Among the boughs, let your joy grow.

Fables of the Forest Floor

In the woods where legends grow,
A wise old owl claims to know.
He spins his tales with great delight,
Of dancing mice that party at night.

Beneath the logs, the mushrooms grin,
Whispering tales of who's been in.
The hedgehogs wear their spiky crowns,
Hosting feasts for forest clowns.

The frogs recite their ribbit song,
While crickets play along, so strong.
A deer pranced through with such finesse,
Only to trip—oh, what a mess!

So gather close, hear nature's cheer,
For in these woods, there's no need to fear.
With laughter shared, our spirits soar,
In fables spun from the forest floor.

The Gnarled Pathway

Through twisted roots and branches wide,
The squirrels scamper, no place to hide.
A raccoon wears a hat just for style,
While turtles ponder, doing it with guile.

The path is crooked, full of quirks,
With bushes whispering, 'Just be the jerk!'
A frog leaps high, then slips in surprise,
Underneath laughter, the critters all rise.

In shadows lurk the woodland sprites,
Dodging the shoes of careless hikes.
They giggle and prance, playing their tricks,
While the owl hoots, "You're such silly pricks!"

A hedgehog grumbles, "Who moved my cheese?"
As ants march by, on unlimited spree.
The gnarled roots dance, a humorous touch,
In this bizarre place, we love just too much.

Veins of the Verdant Vale

In the vale where the laughing leaves sway,
Grass tickles toes at the break of day.
A wandering brook yodels a song,
With fish all dancing, where they belong.

The daisies chat with petals so bright,
About how they missed the last moonlight.
While crickets are critiquing the breeze,
Complaining it's cold, with such a tease.

The mushrooms all gossip while standing tall,
"Did you hear what the willow said to the wall?"
While bees start to buzz with a high-pitched cheer,
Declaring, "We're busy, but glad to be here!"

Oh, the vale is a jolly, wild affair,
Where laughter mingles with fragrant air.
Even the rocks crack jokes by the trail,
Spreading chuckles through the verdant vale.

Fables of the Forest Floor

Among the leaves, a story unfolds,
Where ants tell tales and moss is bold.
A squirrel reads verses from hollowed wood,
And critters all laugh, just as they should.

The beetles disdain their slow-moving fate,
While a wise old owl debates with a crate.
A spider spins webs with a giggling twist,
Creating a net for the flighty mist.

Mice all gather for a raucous feast,
Serving acorns, quite well at least.
The grasshoppers jump to the rhythmic beat,
Making all watch, with their nimble feet.

In shadows of sunbeams, stories enchant,
With chuckles and gasps in a wild chant.
Where fables are spun of laughter and lore,
On the sunny and silly forest floor.

The Breath of the Breathing Wood

In the breathing wood, where echoes play,
Trees gossip with a rustling sway.
A pine may poke a cheeky spruce,
While birches dance, feeling quite loose.

The air is thick with muffled giggles,
As shadows tease with playful wiggles.
A squirrel's joke echoes deep,
Making the stoic oaks leap.

Laughter tumbles down from lofty highs,
Where woodpecker taps become a surprise.
The ferns sway gently, keeping the score,
Of all the funny tales we adore.

Each breath a story we long to share,
In this whimsical world, alive with flair.
Where the breath of the wood brings joy to the air,
And laughter awakens, without a care.

Nature's Heartbeats

In the forest, squirrels play,
Chasing shadows in a fray.
Deer wear antlers, quite a sight,
They look fabulous in soft twilight.

Birds gossip high in the trees,
Singing tales on a summer's breeze.
Each chirp a joke, each caw a laugh,
Nature's humor, a hearty craft.

A rabbit hops, feels pretty grand,
Thinks it's the star of the open land.
While turtles plod in a slow parade,
They take their time, never afraid.

Sunlight dances on leaves of green,
Nature's punchline; it's quite obscene.
Laughter rolls through branches wide,
In the forest, joy can't hide.

In the Shade of Old Growth

Under the branches, shadows weave,
A picnic's planned, we won't believe!
Ants in a line, carrying crumbs,
In their tiny world, each march hums.

A woodpecker knocks like a doorbell chime,
Inviting us to stay for a time.
While wise old owls make witty remarks,
Their wisdom shines like glittering sparks.

Squirrels debate the best acorn stash,
With puffed-out cheeks, they make a splash.
Each old tree holds stories untold,
Of playful secrets and laughter bold.

Shade so thick, it feels like home,
In this wild world, I freely roam.
With every leaf's rustle, the tales combine,
Under the old growth, it's simply divine.

Memories Carved in Wood

Rings of a tree tell tales of yore,
Each year a chapter, never a bore.
Knots like laughter, branches that bend,
Each contour reflects a dear friend.

We carve our names in the forest wide,
With silly smiles that none can hide.
A heart shaped like an oversized shoe,
The trees chuckle as we break through.

Woodpeckers giggle at our designs,
While raccoons raid our picnic lines.
In these moments, humor entwines,
As nature sketches our light-hearted signs.

Time trickles slow, beneath wooden skies,
Where laughter echoes, and spirit flies.
With every hewn mark, life's a jest,
In the great outdoors, we find our best.

Traces of the Timberline

At the timberline, the jokes take flight,
Clouds act silly, oh what a sight!
With trees in rows like marching friends,
Nature's punchlines that never end.

Snowflakes dance, a winter's tease,
Whispering secrets with every breeze.
While llamas ponder the best hat choice,
In their woolly coats, they rejoice.

Traces of laughter, etched in bark,
Each stumble and trip leaves quite a mark.
As mountain streams giggle with glee,
Their sparkling waters, a comedy spree.

With every piked path and cliffside trail,
Fun awaits like a lively tale.
At the timberline, the world unfolds,
In the heart of nature, joy takes hold.

The Lullaby of Lumber

In the forest, trees sway with glee,
Whispering secrets, just you and me.
With logs that dance in the breeze,
They sing us songs that aim to tease.

Bark on bark, a rhythmic tune,
Chop-chop laughter beneath the moon.
Each branch a joke, each leaf a grin,
In the lumberyard, the fun begins!

Shade and shadow, a playful game,
The trees all giggle, calling your name.
Sawdust on the ground, a stage so bright,
Where timber dreams take flight at night.

So cuddle close to your wooden friend,
In this lumber lullaby, there's joy to send.
With every creak and every crack,
The merry wood whispers, "Come on back!"

Stories Carved in Bark

In the woods where stories grow,
Trees tell tales of long ago.
Each notch and swirl, a narrative bright,
Of squirrels and owls in the moonlight.

Carved in bark, a goofy face,
A woodpecker's dance, a funny race.
Bark by bark, the legends tease,
Of mischief managed by the breeze.

With wood and whimsy, the tales unfold,
Of trees that giggle and never grow old.
A family of roots, rooted in fun,
Under the shine of a friendly sun.

So gather 'round for a woodland spree,
Where each tree whispers, "Come, laugh with me!"
In the gallery of green, stories blend,
A barky adventure without an end.

Secrets of the Sapling

Little sapling, what do you know?
Secrets of the forest, do tell, do show.
With big floppy leaves, waving high,
You giggle softly, you cannot lie.

You've seen the squirrels and their tricks,
How they flip and flop, with their funny kicks.
Your roots hear whispers, ancient and wise,
Of a squirrel's mishap and ancient ties.

In your shade, the world holds still,
A party of critters, with time to kill.
Every rustle a riddle, every sound a jest,
In this sapling's safe nook, we find our rest.

So keep your eyes peeled and giggles ready,
For life's a surprise; it's always unsteady.
The secrets you hold, oh, what a delight,
In the world of wonder where laughter's in sight!

Melodies of the Mill

In a bustling mill where wood takes flight,
Machines hum along from morning till night.
With a whir and a clink, they start to play,
A symphony that makes all woes sway.

Logs that tumble, a playful crowd,
Churning out goodies that make us proud.
The saws sing songs of precision divine,
Creating wood wonders, all in a line.

As the chips fly, laughter will rise,
With each little splinter, we're in for a surprise.
Wooden dreams dance through the air,
In this mill of melodies, nothing can compare.

So let the music of wood fill your soul,
Join in the rhythm; lose all control.
In the heart of the mill where laughter does reign,
Life is but woodwork, and joy is the grain!

Whispers of the Weathered Grain

In the quiet woods, trees chuckle so bright,
Their branches sway, a comical sight.
Squirrels gossip, oh what a show,
Whispers of secrets in the breeze that blow.

A log's rolled over, a grin it shows,
Pinecones bounce, as laughter flows.
The oak has a joke, its bark's in a twist,
Nature's stand-up, you can't resist.

Mice wear hats, pulling pranks every day,
Fungi dance whimsically, come join the fray!
Dancing shadows, they all take a spin,
In this forest, the fun won't wear thin.

So hear the giggles, beneath the tall pine,
Life's a hoot, and everything's fine.
With each rustling leaf, let joy unfurl,
Nature's punchline in this playful swirl.

Beneath the Canopy of Dreams

Beneath the leaves, dreams float and soar,
With critters below, ready for more.
A raccoon juggles acorns with flair,
While a wise old owl gasps, 'Did he dare?'

A hedgehog narrates tales of old,
About magic nuts and treasures untold.
The fireflies twinkle like stars in a race,
Illuminating laughter in this silly space.

Bunnies burst in, hopping to the beat,
With hopscotch lines made of twigs at their feet.
They pause to giggle, then leap over logs,
In this dreamy place filled with friendly frogs.

So gather around, hear the stories entwined,
In this wondrous forest where fun's never blind.
The canopy whispers, in chuckles so grand,
Join the whimsy, take a stand!

Echoes in the Sawdust

In the workshop loud, the sawdust flies,
Chips of laughter, beneath the skies.
A hammer taps dance to a rhythmic song,
Sawing through humor where all can't go wrong.

The toolbox grumbles, 'Don't steal my shine!',
While a clamp snaps jokes in perfect line.
The wood insists, 'I'm more than a chair!',
As it wiggles and giggles, a joy to share.

Chisels crack jokes, riveting the night,
Wrenches play games, what a delight!
The lathe spins tales as it whirls round,
Echoes of giggles in this lively ground.

So let the mallet tap to the beat of the fun,
In sawdust romances, let's all get it done.
With every project, the laughter stays near,
In the echoes of wood, you can always cheer!

Heartstrings of the Timberland

In the timberland's heart, laughter's a string,
Tugged by the breeze, it makes the trees sing.
A cricket croons, 'You're flat, oh dear!'
While raccoons join in, shakin' a beer.

The logs are laughing, "We're more than just wood!"
With roots in the earth, all misunderstood.
A squirrel leaps high, with a riddle to share,
"Why was the tree sad? It lost its flair!"

The leaves do a tango, swirling with glee,
While mushrooms boast of their own symphony.
Frogs croak the chorus, in harmony fine,
With each little giggle, the woods intertwine.

Oh timberland laughter, a melody sweet,
With each joyful note, our spirits compete.
So lift up your voices, let's dance through the night,
In heartstrings of nature, the world feels right!

The Symphony of Sycamores

In a grove where whispers dance,
Sycamores chuckle, taking a stance.
A squirrel plays tunes on a twigged flute,
And the wise old owl hoots to the root.

Leaves flutter like giggling sprites,
As branches sway in spontaneous flights.
A raccoon's got rhythm, he taps with glee,
To a beat only the saplings can see.

Even the beetles join in the spree,
With a tap-tap here and a buzz-buzz, whee!
Nature's own band, no need for a score,
Just laughter and music forevermore.

The sun sets low, the concert grows bold,
As fireflies light up, like dreams retold.
In this sweet babble, no heart can be sour,
The symphony thrives in its leafy hour.

Enthralled in Evergreen

Underneath the evergreens tall,
A hedgehog tells tales, quite amusing to all.
He spins wild stories of moonlit escapades,
While the magpies giggle and toss their braids.

A pine cone declares it's a knight of the wood,
With acorns as armor, as brave as they could.
The ferns all nod, with their bright green fronds,
In a forest where humor forever responds.

A bear in a bowtie begins a charade,
While rabbits applaud, feeling quite overpaid.
A porcupine dances with style and grace,
With a wig made of grass that covers his face.

Oh, the joy of the trees, the mirth in the air,
Where a laugh is a leaf, free-floating everywhere.
In evergreens' charm, we find such delight,
A rollicking jig through the cool, starry night.

The Forest's Eternal Verse

In a meadow of musings where shadows will play,
The flowers have secrets they whisper all day.
A bee in a top hat, quite certain of flair,
Sips nectar like VIPs at a fancy affair.

The sunflowers gossip, their heads held up high,
While the crickets perform their fresh night lullaby.
A deer with a monocle surveys with great cheer,
Crafting a sonnet, adding rhyme without fear.

The breeze sings a tune that weaves through the leaves,
Tickling the branches like a child who believes.
Each rustle a chuckle, each rustle a grin,
Nature's own laughter where wonders begin.

So dance with the shadows, waltz with the light,
Join the joyous verses of forest delight.
In this whimsical world, together we'll weave,
A tapestry woven of joy to believe.

The Legend of Lichen

In the tale of a lichen, so sticky and sly,
It claims to be ready for a waltz in the sky.
But the stones just chuckle, and the moss rolls its eyes,
As the lichen insists, it's the star of the pies.

"Lichens are lovers of sunshine and rain,
I'm the chef of the forest! Just taste my terrain."
While beetles all chuckle and bees hum along,
The trees sway in rhythm, they know he's not wrong.

With a patchy complexion, both green and both gray,
He ordered a banquet of leaves for the day.
"A salad, a stir-fry, a spread so divine,
With snacks from the squirrels and grapes from the vine!"

So when winter comes knocking, and the snow fluffs the floor,
Remember the legend, the laughter, the lore.
For even in stillness, there's fun to be found,
In the stories of lichen that twirl round and round.

www.ingramcontent.com/pod-product-compliance
Lightning Source LLC
Chambersburg PA
CBHW071824160426
43209CB00003B/199